My First Money Adventure
How to Save for Big Dreams!

Alina Salabin
MONEY PREP ACADEMY

About Money Prep Academy

Money Prep Academy, based in the heart of Glastonbury, Somerset, UK, is committed to delivering practical and accessible financial education and is specialized in equipping individuals and families with the tools they need to take control of their financial futures. From building emergency funds to planning for major life goals like buying a home or saving for retirement, our mission is to simplify personal finance and empower people to achieve financial stability and success.

Our website,

ww.moneyprepacademy.co.uk,

serves as a resource hub where you can find valuable tips, guides, and online courses tailored to all stages of your financial journey.

Table of Contents

1. **Chapter 1: My First Money Adventure** 5

Leo's Big Dream: Saving for the Space Museum

Activity: Plan Your Own Adventure

Jokes Time!

2. **Chapter 2: Building an Emergency Fund** ………………………………….......... 17

Why Do You Need an Emergency Fund?

Story: Leo Learns About the Emergency Fund

Activity: Build Your Own Emergency Fund

Jokes Time!

3. **Chapter 3: Saving for a Home** 27

What is a Down Payment?

Story: Leo's Big Dream of a Home

Activity: Build Your Dream Purchase

Jokes Time!

4. **Chapter 4: Saving for Other Big Goals** 36

How to Set a Savings Goal

Activity: Build Your Dream Purchase

Jokes Time!

5. **Chapter 5: Staying Motivated** 42

MY FIRST MONEY ADVENTURE
How to Save for Big Dreams!

Tips for Staying Motivated

Story: Leo's Mission to Save for a Robotic LEGO Set

Activity: Stay Motivated with Your Savings

Jokes Time!

6. **Chapter 6: Practical Ways to Save Money** 53

Easy Tips for Saving Money

Working with Your Parents to Save

7. **Chapter 7: Setting Long-Term and Short-Term Goals** ………………………………… 61

Difference Between Short-Term and Long-Term Goals

Story: Leo Saves for Tennis Camp

8. **Chapter 8: Learning the Importance of Patience** …………………………………….. 68

Why is Patience Important in Saving?

Activity: Track Your Progress and Stay Focused

Jokes Time!

9. **Conclusion: Small Steps to Big Goals** 74

Recap of What You've Learned

MY FIRST MONEY ADVENTURE
How to Save for Big Dreams!

MY FIRST MONEY ADVENTURE
How to Save for Big Dreams!

CHAPTER 1

My First Money Adventure: How to Save for Big Dreams!

This book will teach you how to save money for important goals, like an emergency fund, a new home, or other big dreams.

Along the way, you'll learn how to plan your savings step-by-step, understand just how important is having a savings strategy, and use simple tips to save money over time.

Having a strategy means having a very good plan to do something very special to you.

Always remember to ask your parents or guardians if you don't understand something or need any help.

Why are Savings Important?

Saving money helps you feel safe and secure. Imagine if you suddenly needed to fix something or pay for something important, if you have saved enough money, you won't need to worry.

Saving is also important if you have a big dream, like buying your own house, going on a trip, or maybe starting a business when you grow up.

A business is when people make money by selling things or providing services that others need. For example, if you run a lemonade stand, you buy lemons and sugar, make lemonade, and sell it to people for more than it cost you to make. The extra money you keep is called profit.

And that will be called your business.

Saving money isn't just about having a lot of money, it's about having a plan. No matter how much you earn or get as pocket money, you can learn how to save and grow your money. And you can do this having a plan.

Why Do You Need a Plan?

Let's think of having saved some money as a journey you do. You wouldn't go on a trip without knowing where you're going, right?

It's the same with saving, you need a plan. It helps you know exactly what you want to achieve, how much you need, and how to get there.

But don't worry, we'll break it all down into simple steps. And if you need help understanding anything, ask your parents to show you examples or explain how they do it!

Summary

This book will teach you how to save money for important goals, like an emergency fund, a new home, or other big dreams.

Along the way, you'll learn how to plan your savings step-by-step.

You will maybe understand the importance of having a savings strategy and use simple tips to save money over time.

Story:

Leo's Big Dream

Leo had a big dream, he wanted to go on a special trip to visit a space museum. But he knew that trips like these cost money, so he needed a plan to save up.

One day, his mom told him, "Leo, if you want to reach a big goal, like visiting the space museum, you need to have a savings plan. Think of it like an adventure, and every time you save, you get one step closer to your dream."

Leo smiled; he could already imagine himself being there. Excited, Leo grabbed a notebook and wrote down how much money he needed for the trip. "Okay!" he thought, "if I save £5 every week from my allowance, I can reach my goal in six months!"

Week by week, Leo put aside his £5 into a special jar he labelled "Space Museum Fund."

At first, it seemed like it would take forever, but his mom reminded him, "Every little bit is counting, Leo! You're building your dream step by step, one penny at the time."

Leo also found clever ways to save money, like packing his own lunch for school instead of buying snacks and choosing to borrow books from the library instead of buying new ones. After a few months, his jar was half full, and Leo felt proud. He realized that saving wasn't just about having money, it was about having a plan and sticking to it.

Finally, after six months, Leo reached his goal!

He had saved enough to visit the space museum. As he stood in front of a giant rocket ship on his trip and he smiled as he knew that his savings adventure had helped him reach the stars, one small step at a time. And he made it possible!

Activity Time: Plan Your Own Adventure!

What's your big dream? Just like Leo saved for his trip to the space museum, now it's your turn to plan for something exciting.

Draw your dream: Use this space to draw what you're saving for, maybe it's a toy, a trip, or a special event.

MY FIRST MONEY ADVENTURE
How to Save for Big Dreams!

How much will it cost? Write down how much money you need to reach your goal:

Cost of your dream: £_____

_____
_____
_____
_____
_____

Make a plan: How much can you save each week?

I will save £_____ every week.

Calculate the time: Now, divide the total cost of your dream by how much you plan to save each week. That's how many weeks it will take to reach your goal!

It will take me _____ weeks to save enough!

Jokes Time!

Let's have a little fun!

Question 1. Why did the money go to school?

Answer: Because it wanted to make more cents!

Question 2. What did the piggy bank say to the cash?

Answer: Don't worry, I've got you covered!

CHAPTER 2

Building an Emergency Fund.

An emergency fund is money you save for when something unexpected happens, like needing to fix your bike or buy new school supplies.

This money helps you feel safe because you have it ready when you need it.

An emergency fund is like a special piggy bank that you don't touch unless something really important or maybe something unexpected happens.

For example, if your bike breaks and you need to fix it, or if you need new clothes because you've outgrown your old ones. The emergency fund helps you pay for these things without asking for extra money.

Why do you even need an emergency fund?

Think of it this way: if you were playing outside and suddenly your shoes got torn, you would need new shoes right away. If you have an emergency fund, you could buy the shoes without having to worry.

It's always good to have money set aside for when life surprises you.

Ask your parents to help you write down the things your family spends money on each month. That way, you can understand how much they need for their emergency fund, and why it's important.

How much do you need?

To build a good emergency fund, you need to know how much your family spends on things like food, rent, or clothes each month.

Most families try to save enough to cover 3 moths to 6 months of expenses. For example, if your family spends £1000 per month, they will want to save around £3000 for 3 months and to £6000 for six months for the family`s emergency fund.

Ask your parents to show you how they calculate their monthly expenses and why they save for emergencies.

Story:

Leo Learns About what is the Emergency Fund

Leo had just come back from his amazing trip to the space museum when something unexpected has just happened, suddenly his favourite backpack tore apart! The zipper broke, and the straps were coming loose. Leo needed a new one for school, but he hadn't planned for this.

His mom noticed the torn backpack and said, "Leo, this is why we have something called an emergency fund. It's money we save just for times like this, when something unexpected happens."

Leo was curious. "What's an emergency fund?"

"It's like a special piggy bank you don't touch unless something really important comes up," his mom explained.

"You save this money in case you need it for things like fixing a car or, in your case, buying a new backpack."

Leo thought about it. "So, it's like saving for things you didn't expect, right?"

"Exactly!" his mom said smiling. "When you have an emergency fund, you don't have to worry if something surprising happens because you've already saved money to take care of it."

Leo decided to start his own emergency fund.

Every week, he saved a little bit of his allowance, just like he did when he was saving for the space museum trip. Soon, Leo had enough money in his emergency fund to buy without any worries a new bike that just broke in that weekend.

He realized how smart it was to have savings set aside for surprises.

Now, Leo didn't just have a plan for big dreams, he also had a plan for life's serious surprises.

Activity Time: Build Your Own Emergency Fund!

Just like Leo learned about having an emergency fund, now it's time for you to plan your own!

MY FIRST MONEY ADVENTURE
How to Save for Big Dreams!

Draw your emergency fund jar: Imagine you have your own emergency fund. Use this space to draw what your emergency jar looks like—maybe you can even label it "Emergency Fund."

What would you save for? Write down some things you might need to use your emergency fund for:

MY FIRST MONEY ADVENTURE
How to Save for Big Dreams!

Fixing my _____

_____

_____

_____

_____

_____(e.g., bike or toy)

Buying new _____

_____

_____

_____

_____

_____ (e.g., school supplies or what do you need?)

Set a goal: How much would you like to save for your emergency fund?

My emergency fund goal is: £_____

Make a plan: How much can you save each week to reach your emergency goal?

I will save £_____ every week.

Jokes Time!

Let's have a laugh! Here are two more jokes to keep things light while you save:

1 Question: Why did the coin bring a ladder to the bank?

Answer: Because it wanted to climb to the top savings!

2. Question: What do you call a piggy bank that's empty?

Answer: Un-fortune-ate!

CHAPTER 3

Saving for a Home:

When saving for a home, you need to save a lot of money for a "down payment." This is the money you pay upfront to own a house. The more you save, the easier it will be to buy your own home one day.

When you think about your future, one of the big goals many people have is to own a home.

What is a down payment?

Imagine you wanted to buy a new video game, but it costs a lot. You might save up some of your allowance first and ask your parents to cover the rest. The part you save is like a down payment, it's the money you pay before you can get something bigger, like a house.

Ask your parents to explain how much houses cost in your area and how they saved up for their home.

This will help you understand why saving for a home takes time but is worth it.

The "down payment" is a part of the money you pay upfront when you buy the house.

The more you save for the down payment, the less money you'll need to borrow.

"Borrow" means to take money from someone, like a bank, that you promise to pay back later. When you borrow money, you use it now but must give it back over time, usually with some extra money added as a fee for borrowing. For example, if you don't have enough to buy a house, you might borrow some money

from the bank and pay it back little by little.

Draw Your Dream Purchase!
Use the space below to draw a picture of the cool item you would like to save for!

How to start saving for a home

Saving for a home starts with knowing how much homes cost.

Imagine you want to buy a house that costs £200,000. To get the house, you need to pay part of the money upfront, kind of like when you buy something at a store but only pay a little bit first.

For example, if the house costs £200,000, you might need to save between £20,000 and £40,000 before you can buy it.

The more you save, the less you need to borrow from the bank to pay for the rest.

You don't need to save it all at once. You can start by saving a little each month and watching your savings grow.

Ask your parents to help you understand how much they saved each month for their home and how long it took them to save for the down payment.

Story:

Leo's Big Dream of a Home

One afternoon, Leo was talking to his mom about the future. "Mom, when I grow up, I want to buy my own house! How do people do that!? Houses cost a lot, right?"

His mom smiled gently. "Yes, they do, Leo! That's why people usually save money for something called a "down payment". It's the money you pay upfront when you buy a house. The more you save, the less you'll need to borrow from the bank."

Leo's eyes widened. "Borrow? What does 'borrow' mean?"

His mom explained, "Borrowing means taking money from someone, like a bank, and promising to pay it back over time. But you don't just give back the exact amount you borrowed. You also have to pay a little extra as a fee for borrowing the money."

Leo thought for a moment. "Banks really give you so much money, like enough money to buy a house? Why do they do that?"

His mom smiled softly and said, "Yes, banks lend money to help people buy houses, cars, or other big things they can't afford to pay for all at once. They do this because they know people will pay the money back little by little over time, with the extra fee as their profit. That's how banks earn money."

Leo's curiosity grew. "If the bank gives me so much money, why do they need a down payment from me? Can't they just lend me all of it?"

His mom nodded kindly, that was a really good question, and she said:

"Good question, Leo! The bank asks for a down payment to make sure you're serious about buying the house and that you have some of your own money saved up. It also means you won't need to borrow as much from them. The more you save for the down payment, the less you'll need to borrow, and the easier it will be to pay the money back."

Leo was fascinated. "So, if a house costs £200,000, and I save up a big down payment, I won't need to borrow as much, and that's a good thing?"

"That's right," his mom said. "If you save £20,000 to £40,000, you'll only need to borrow the rest. And saving a little each month helps a lot over time, just like when you saved for your trip to the space museum."

Leo smiled, feeling proud. "I get it now! Saving for a house is a big goal, but if I start small and save step by step, I can make it happen one day."

His mom gave him a gentle hug. "Exactly, Leo. One penny at a time. Saving for big dreams, like your own home, takes time, but with patience and a plan, you'll get there, my little sweetie sweetheart!"

CHAPTER 4

Saving for Other Big Goals

Sometimes we have other big dreams that we want to save for. It could be a trip to a special place, buying a new bike, or even starting a small business one day.

For these big goals, just like with a house, you need to save step by step.

How to set a savings goal

First, think about what you want. Let's say you want to buy a new bike that costs £500. You don't have all the money right away.

You can save £50 each month, and after 10 months, you'll have enough to buy the bike! Because 10 times 50 equals 500, right?

Ask your parents to help you figure out how much you should save each month for your goal, whether it's a bike, a trip, or something else important to you.

Activity Time: Build Your Dream Purchase!

Let's play a fun game where you can make your dream purchase by saving up for a down payment and borrowing the rest from the "Bank of Mum and Dad!"

Pick Your Dream Purchase: Imagine you want to buy something super fun, like a *new bike, cool video game,* or *giant stuffed animal.*

My dream purchase will be:

_____
_____
_____
_____
_____
_____
_____
_____

Spin the Wheel: Let's imagine the total cost of your dream item!

Spin the *imaginary wheel* to land on a price:

- ✓ £100
- ✓ £150
- ✓ £200

Total cost of my item: £_____

Roll for Your Down Payment: You get to decide how much of the total price you can pay! Roll a dice (or pick a number from 1 to 6) to figure out your down payment!

Each number on the dice represents how much you'll save (multiplied by £20):

- ✓ **Rolled 1** = £20
- ✓ **Rolled 2** = £40

✓ **Rolled 3** = £60

✓ **Rolled 4** = £80

✓ **Rolled 5** = £100

✓ **Rolled 6** = £120

My down payment: £_____

Borrow from the Bank of Mum and Dad: Now that you've saved some money, you'll need to borrow the rest.

What's left to borrow: £_____
(Total cost - Down payment)

The "Bank of Mum and Dad" will lend you this money, but you have to pay it back!

Payback Challenge!

How fast can you pay off your loan? Choose how much you'll

pay each week (or month) by completing a fun challenge! Every time you do something awesome—like *helping with chores*, *doing homework*, or *being extra nice*—you can pay £10 back!

My payback plan: £10 each week/month for _____ weeks/months.

Jokes Time!

1. Question: Why did the piggy bank go to the doctor?
Answer: Because it felt a little broke!

2. Question: Why did the banker switch careers?
Answer: He lost interest!

CHAPTER 5

Staying Motivated

Saving money can sometimes be hard, especially when you see things you really want to buy.

Maybe you want a new game, or your friends are spending money on other fun but expensive things.

It's okay to feel like you want to spend, but it's also important to stick to your savings plan.

What challenges might you face?

One of the hardest things about saving is waiting.

Imagine you are saving for a new bike, and it costs £500, but after three months, you only have £150, because three months means 3 times 50, as you manage to put 50 aside in your saving jar.

It might feel like you'll never get there, and you might even feel like giving up. This is normal!

But remember, saving takes time, and every bit you save brings you closer to your goal.

Another challenge could be spending money on small things, like snacks or toys.

These little things can add up and make it harder to save.

It's okay to buy something fun sometimes, but always think about your big goal first.

Ask your parents if they have faced challenges while saving and how they stayed motivated. You can learn from their experience!

MY FIRST MONEY ADVENTURE
How to Save for Big Dreams!

Tips to stay motivated

Set small goals: Instead of only thinking about the big goal, set small milestones.

For example, if you are saving for a bike, first aim to save £100, then £200, and so on. Every time you reach a small goal, you'll feel proud of yourself.

Celebrate your progress: When you hit a savings milestone, reward yourself with something small, like a treat or an extra playtime.

This makes saving more fun!

Keep a savings tracker: Make a chart to show how much you've saved. Seeing your progress grow will keep you excited to save more.

Story:

Leo's Mission to Save for a Robotic LEGO Set

Leo's latest passion was building with LEGO. He loved creating all kinds of things, but there was one set that he really, really wanted, the **Robotic LEGO Set**.

It could move, make sounds, and even respond to commands! But there was one big problem: it costs £300, and Leo didn't have that much money.

Determined, Leo started saving. Every month, he put £30 into his savings jar, dreaming of the day he could finally build his robot. After three months, he checked his jar and saw £90.

"Ugh!" Leo muttered, feeling a little discouraged.

"I still need £210. It feels like I'll never have enough to buy the LEGO set."

His mom noticed he looked frustrated and sat next to him. "What's on your mind, Leo?"

"I've been saving for months, but I still have so far to go. It's hard when I see my friends buying new LEGO sets and other fun things. It makes me want to spend my money now," Leo admitted.

His mom smiled gently. "I understand, Leo. Saving can be tough, especially when it feels like you're waiting forever. But remember, saving is like building with LEGO, one piece at a time. You're already making great progress!"

"But it feels so slow!" Leo sighed frustrated and sad.

"How about we make it more fun?" his mom suggested.

"Instead of only thinking about the £300 you need, why don't you set smaller goals? First aim for £100, then £150, and so on. That way, you'll feel proud each time you reach a smaller milestone."

Leo's eyes lit up. "That sounds like a good idea! Maybe I could reward myself when I hit the £100 goal." He knew he is having already £90, and thinking to a good reward made him smile.

"Exactly!" his mom said. "When you save £100, you could get a small treat, like a new LEGO figure, or have extra time to play with your current sets. It'll help you so you will keep being, hopefully, excited to save more."

"And I could make a chart to track my savings!" Leo said excitedly. "That way, I can see how close I'm getting to my robotic LEGO set!"

"Perfect idea, darling" his mom said. "Every time you add to your savings, colour in your chart and watch how much closer you're getting to your goal."

Feeling motivated again, Leo grabbed some paper and coloured pencils and made a chart for his Robotic LEGO Set Savings.

He even decorated it with pictures of LEGO bricks and robots. With each small milestone he hit, Leo felt proud and knew he was getting closer to building his dream robot.

"I can do this!" Leo thought, feeling more determined than ever.

Saving was just like building with LEGO, it took time, but piece by piece, he would get there.

Activity Time: Stay Motivated with Your Savings!

Saving money can feel slow sometimes, but don't worry! Let's make it more fun with a **Savings Challenge!**

Create a Rewards Chart: Every time you reach a small savings goal, you get a reward! Draw five steps on your savings chart, like a staircase, leading up to your big goal at the top. For each step you reach, give yourself a fun reward!

Step 1: Save £20

Reward: _____ (e.g., extra playtime, a favourite snack)

Step 2: Save £40

Reward: _____

Step 3: Save £60

Reward: _____

Step 4: Save £80

Reward: _____

Step 5: Reach your big savings goal! £100

Reward _____

Decorate Your Savings Jar:

Make your savings jar exciting! Draw or use stickers to decorate it, reminding you of what you're saving for. You could add pictures of your dream toy, trip, or special event on it!

Track Your Progress:

Every time you add money to your jar, colour in a part of your **Savings Tracker**. You can make a chart or a thermometer drawing to show how close you're getting to your big goal! Seeing the progress will keep you motivated.

CHAPTER 6

Practical Ways to Save Money

Saving money doesn't mean you have to stop having fun! It just means you need to be smart about where your money goes.

Here are some easy ways you can save money, even if you're still getting pocket money or small amounts from doing chores.

1. Make a savings jar

You can start by creating a special jar or box where you keep your savings.

Every time you get money, put some of it in the jar.

You can even decorate it and label it with your goal, like "Bike Fund" or "Holiday Fund." This way, you'll always remember what you're saving for.

2. Save a little every week

Even if you only save a small amount, like £2 or £5 a week, it adds up.

Let's say you save £5 every week for 10 weeks. How much do you think that will be?

Exactly, you'll have £50 by the end!

Ask your parents to help you decide how much of your pocket money you can put into savings each week.

3. Think before you buy

Before you buy something, ask yourself: "Do I really need this right now?" Sometimes, it's better to save that money for your bigger goal.

It's okay to treat yourself sometimes, but don't let small expenses to stop you from reaching your savings goal.

Ask your parents if they also save a little each week and how they decide what to spend money on and what to save.

4. Working with Your Parents

Sometimes saving money can be easier when you have someone to help you.

Your parents, your aunt or your uncle, your grandparents, can be great partners in saving! They can help you set goals, track your progress, and give you advice on how to reach your savings target.

How can your parents help you save?

They can match your savings: Some parents might offer to "match" the money you save. This means if you save £10, they will add £10 to your savings. Ask your parents if they can help you in this way. It is ok if they don`t agree, but if they do it's a great way to reach your goal faster!

They can give you tips: Your parents know a lot about saving money. Ask them for advice on how they saved for big things, like buying a car or going on vacation.

You can learn a lot from their experience.

Story:

Leo's Smart Saving Tips for His Robotic LEGO Set

Leo was still on his mission to save for the **Robotic LEGO Set**, and while he was excited, he knew he needed to be smart with his money if he wanted to reach his goal faster. His mom had already shared some great tips with him, so he decided to try them out.

One day, Leo took a plain jar from the kitchen and started decorating it.

He drew colourful robots and LEGO bricks all over it and labelled it "**Robotic LEGO Fund**."

Every time he got his pocket money or received some from

family, he'd put a part of it in his special jar.

"Saving a little bit each week really adds up," Leo thought to himself. "Even if I only save £5 a week, I'll have £50 in just 10 weeks!"

But Leo also knew he had to be careful with how he spent his money. One afternoon, he was at the toy store with his friends, and he saw a cool mini-LEGO set he wanted to buy right away.

"Hmm," Leo thought. "Do I really need this right now, or should I save for the Robotic LEGO Set?"

He remembered what his mom had told him about thinking before buying. He decided to wait and keep saving for his big goal. "I'll feel so much better when I finally get my robotic set," Leo reminded himself, putting the mini set back on the shelf.

At home, Leo talked to his mom about how to save even better.

"Mom, do you think you could help me save by matching what I save?"

His mom smiled. "I think that's a great idea, Leo! If you save £10, I'll add £10 to your fund. But remember, you're doing most of the work by saving a little each week."

Leo was thrilled. "Thanks, Mom! That'll help me get my LEGO set even faster."

As the weeks passed, Leo stuck to his plan. He saved part of his pocket money each week and added it to his decorated jar.

His mom matched his savings from time to time, and together, they tracked his progress on a chart he had hung on the wall. Little by little, Leo saw his savings grow.

One day, when Leo checked his jar, he realized he was closer to his goal than ever.

All of his smart saving, careful spending, and the help from his mom had paid off. Soon, he'd be able to buy his dream Robotic LEGO Set and build the coolest robot ever!

My, Gosh! He was so happy!

CHAPTER 7

Setting Long-Term and Short-Term Goals

When you're saving money, it's important to understand the difference between short-term and long-term goals.

This helps you know which goals you can reach quickly, and which ones will take more time and patience.

What are short-term goals?

Short-term goals are things you can save for and buy in a short amount of time, like within a few weeks or months.

These might include buying a new toy, going to the cinema with friends, or saving up for a special event like a birthday gift.

Let's say you want to save £30 to buy a new game. If you save £5 each week, you'll be able to buy the game in six weeks! That's a short-term goal.

What are long-term goals?

Long-term goals take more time to achieve, usually a year or more.

These could be big things like saving for a bike, a new computer, or even your first car when you're older.

It might take you months or even years to save enough, but with patience and a good plan, you can get there.

For example, if you want to save £300 for a new bike and you can save £10 a week, it will take you 30 weeks to reach your goal. That's a long-term goal.

Ask your parents to help you set both short-term and long-term goals.

You can work together to figure out how much you need to save each week or month for each goal.

This way, you can always keep track of your progress.

Story: Leo Saves for Tennis Camp

Leo loved tennis. He spent hours playing with his friends at the park, imagining himself playing in big tournaments one day.

So, when his coach told him about a **tennis summer camp**, Leo's eyes lit up. The camp was for a whole week, with real coaches and special training sessions. But there was one problem, it wasn't cheap.

Leo rushed home to tell his parents. His mom smiled and said, "That sounds like an amazing opportunity, Leo! But it's going to cost quite a bit. How about we help you with part of it, but you'll need to save for the rest?"

Leo was excited but a little nervous. He hadn't saved for something this big before.

But he was determined. This wasn't just about getting a toy or a game, this was about doing something he *loved*.

Plus, going to the camp would help him improve his tennis skills, and Leo knew it was worth it.

So, Leo grabbed an old jar and labelled it **"Tennis Camp Fund"**.

He figured out that if he saved £100 a week for a few months, he'd have enough to cover his part of the camp fee.

His parents promised to match whatever he saved, but the rest was up to him.

Each week, Leo set aside some of his allowance, but he also found extra ways to earn money.

He helped his neighbour wash her car, mowed his grandparents' lawn, and even sold some of his old toys that he didn't use anymore.

At first, it felt like it would take forever.

One weekend, Leo and his friends went to the mall, and Leo saw a brand-new video game he really wanted. *"Maybe I could just spend a little of my savings,"* he thought. But then he remembered how much he wanted to go to the tennis camp.

That night, Leo sat down at his desk and looked at his **Tennis Camp Fund** jar.

He pulled out his savings tracker and filled in the next line on his chart. He could see he was getting closer to his goal, and that felt better than the video game ever could.

Finally, after weeks of saving and hard work, Leo reached his goal! His jar was full, and he was ready for tennis camp.

When his parents saw how much effort he had put into saving, they were proud to match his contribution.

At camp, Leo learned new skills, made friends, and had the best week ever.

As he played his final game at camp, he thought about how his patience and hard work had paid off. *"This was worth every penny,"* Leo thought with a smile as he hit another winning shot.

CHAPTER 8

Learning the Importance of Patience

One of the most important things about saving is patience. It can be tough to wait when you want something right away, but learning to be patient will help you reach your savings goals faster and make the reward even more special.

Why is patience important when saving?

Let's imagine you're saving for a big goal, like a new bike. It might take a long time to save enough money, and sometimes you might feel like spending your savings on something smaller, like a toy or a treat.

But if you stay patient and keep saving, you'll have enough for that bike in no time!

Patience helps you stay focused on your big goals and not get distracted by smaller things along the way.

How can you practice patience?

Remind yourself of your goal: Keep a picture or drawing of what you're saving for. This will help you remember why you're saving and keep you excited about reaching your goal.

Track your progress: Use a savings tracker where you can colour in or fill up a chart each time you save more money. Seeing your progress can help you stay patient and motivated.

Talk to your parents: Ask your parents how they practice patience when saving for something big.

They can share tips with you on how to stay focused and avoid spending money on smaller things.

Small Savings, Big Rewards

Sometimes, it's easy to think that saving a little bit of money each week won't make a big difference. But when you save small amounts regularly, they add up!

Let's look at a few simple examples of things you can buy by saving small amounts.

Ask your parents to help you if you need. It's fun to see your money grow!

Example: Saving for a Toy

Imagine you want a new toy that costs £25. You earn £5 a week from doing small chores around the house. If you save £3 every week, in about 8 weeks you'll be able to buy the toy!

Cost of the toy: £25

Saving each week: £3

Make the math and you will see that the resulted time to reach your goal is 8 weeks.

Example 2: Saving for a Trip to the Cinema

You want to go to the cinema with your friends. A movie ticket costs £12. If you save £2 each week from your allowance, in 6 weeks you'll have enough for your ticket!

Cost of the movie ticket: £12

Saving each week: £2

Time to reach your goal: 6 weeks

Small Steps to Big Goals

As you can see, even saving just a little bit each week helps you reach your goals faster than you might think.

It's all about staying patient and consistent.

Remember, the key is to start small, save regularly, and keep track of your progress!

Ask your parents to help you create a chart or savings tracker so you can see how your money grows.

It's exciting to watch your small amounts turn into big rewards!

Conclusion and Next Steps

Congratulations! You've learned how to set savings goals, stay patient, and make small savings add up to big rewards.

Whether you're saving for a toy, a bike, or even something big in the future like a car, or your first home, you now have the tools to make it happen.

Remember, saving is all about consistency, about having patience, and staying focused on your goals. About having a plan, remember?

What did you learn?

- How to set short-term and long-term goals.
- How to overcome challenges and stay motivated.
- Practical ways to save small amounts and make them grow over time.

The next time you get some pocket money or earn a little for doing chores, think about how much closer you are to your dream goals.

Every coin you save brings you one step closer to what you want!

One Penny at a Time

The End

About the Author

Alina Salabin is the founder and lead instructor at Money Prep Academy.

With a diverse professional background spanning law, finance, governance, risk management, and digital transformation, Alina is uniquely qualified to offer financial guidance rooted in real-world experience and best practices.

Alina holds qualifications in law and accounting, business, digital transformation and leadership. She worked as an accountant since 2015, provided tax advice since 2018, and has served as a Money Laundering Reporting Officer (MLRO) since 2020.

As a Fellow member of the ICA, FICA, International Compliance

Association, Alina brings a wealth of experience to her work, and her passion for simplifying finance inspired the creation of Money Prep Academy.

Through Money Prep Academy, Alina's mission is to help individuals and families who may feel overwhelmed by finance by breaking down difficult concepts into simple steps.

Through her work, Alina aims to make simple most complex concepts about personal finance, enabling people to take control of their financial futures with confidence.

Money Prep Academy® Ltd Money Prep Academy is registered in England and Wales under CRN 15169086.

Disclaimer:

The information provided in this book, including any recommendations of tools, resources, or books, is for general informational and educational purposes only.

Money Prep Academy® Ltd *and the author,* ***Alina Salabin****, are not affiliated with any of the products, companies, or authors mentioned in this book, and we do not receive any financial compensation for their inclusion. The recommendations are based solely on our independent assessment and should not be construed as endorsements.*

While we strive to provide accurate and up-to-date information, personal finance is a complex subject, and every individual's financial situation is unique. The content in this book does not constitute financial, legal, or tax advice. We encourage readers to consult with another qualified professional for advice tailored to their specific circumstances.

Money Prep Academy® Ltd *and the author cannot be held responsible for any actions taken based on the information provided in this book, nor for any losses, legal liabilities, or other consequences that may result. By using the information in this book, you agree that you are solely responsible for your financial decisions.*

Continue Your Financial Journey with Money Prep Academy

At Money Prep Academy® Ltd, our mission is to help individuals and families take control of their finances and build a secure future. Our books are designed to provide simple, actionable advice that empowers you to make smart financial decisions and don't hesitate to reach out with questions or feedback. We're here to support you every step of the way.

Thank you for your time and for choosing Money Prep Academy®

www.moneyprepacademy.co.uk

MY FIRST MONEY ADVENTURE
How to Save for Big Dreams!

Printed in Great Britain
by Amazon

38d16f64-4470-4e1c-a4d1-4154b6f980ddR01